# THE SUN, THE SHADOW, AND THE SILENCE

# THE SUN, THE SHADOW, AND THE SILENCE

R. DORIAN NIGHT

J MERRILL

J MERRILL

Published by J Merrill Publishing, Inc.
2323 W 5th Ave., Suite 120
Columbus, OH 43204
www.JMerrill.pub

Paperback ISBN-13: 978-1-961475-55-7
eBook ISBN-13: 978-1-961475-56-4

Book Title: The Sun, The Shadow, and The Silence
Author: R. Dorian Night

Printed in the United States of America
[First Edition]

*For my Family*

# PART I

## THE SUN

# 1

## A BEACON IN THE NIGHT

In midnight's hush, where shadows creep,
I find thee waking, yet lost in sleep.
Thy smile, a beacon, soft and bright,
A star that cleaves the endless night.

Thou call'st me fair, yet blind art thee,
For all the light doth dwell in thee.
No grand design, no lover's plea,
But simple mirth, 'twixt thee and me.

My words do flow as rivers wide,
Yet seek not chains, nor wish to bide.
If doubts do cloud thy troubled sight,
I stand but near, a steadfast light.

Thy voice, a balm, thy laughter pure,
A solace rare, a bond secure.
Amidst false tongues that feign and lie,
I stand in truth—no mask, no sigh.

Once, drawn by beauty's fleeting spell,
But now by kindness bound as well.
A whispered verse, an ode so slight,
To friendship's glow, not passion's blight.

No tethered heart, no yearning woe,
Just moments shared in moon's soft glow.
Forgive my faults, my clinging way,
I seek not more, nor bid thee stay.

If walls do rise, then let them stand,
No forceful touch, no grasping hand.
For love's cruel jest I do not weave,
I wait, I listen—I do not grieve.

So let the names fade into mist,
Yet laughter linger, light and crisp.
Through fleeting time and fate's decree,
This bond remains—serene and free.

## 2

# A LOVER'S FAREWELL

Ah, blessed be the hand that tore,
For I could ne'er have closed that door.
Bound was I, a wretched slave,
To love's sweet gift—a gilded grave.

Thy peace was but a fleeting breath,
A whisper soft that welcomed death.
Yet still I drank, my opium sweet,
Though ruin lapped at weary feet.

I knew, I knew—I must let go,
Yet clutched thee close, as tides do woe.
A drug, a curse, a siren's call,
I longed to flee—yet longed for all.

Once, dear heart, I called thee rare,
And placed thee high with tender care.
Yet now, as friend, must match thy tone,
No longer worship at thy throne.

So chide me not when eyes do read,
Yet lips grow silent, cold, and freed.
For I have seen the trembling hands,
The fleeting glances, tight-bound strands.

A tongue that falters in the crowd,
A name unspoken, yet still loud.
What proof need I of love's demise,
When silence shrouds thy knowing eyes?

Ah, fickle fate—thou didst bestow
A love that burned, yet chilled as snow.
Wouldst thou keep names that once held fire,
Yet cast aside the true desire?

Fear thee not—my heart lies still,
Resigned unto thy quiet kill.
For long I've known, as shadows creep,
That love like ours was ne'er to keep.

So, part we must, as strangers might,
No war, no wail—just faded light.
Yet if the years do steal our breath,
I'll wonder, love, what still is left.

# 3

## WHISPERS IN THE VOID

I wish for gold, for gilded fame,
For all the world to know my name.
But what is wealth when shadows creep,
And demons wake me from my sleep?

Dost thou know the weight of sorrow—
The dread of nights that yield no morrow?
The bitter war 'twixt life and death,
Each sigh, each gasp, each stolen breath?

Hast thou juggled fate's cruel jest,
A fleeting hope, a hollow test?
To live, to smile, to mask the pain,
While ghosts still whisper and remain?

O cursed fate, so swift, so cold,
To rip away what hands can't hold.
To steal the ground from 'neath my tread,
To leave me standing with the dead.

Yet lo, though darkness grips thee tight,
The dawn still stirs beyond the night.
Seasons change, the winds do call—
Even shadows one day fall.

Think thee lost? Nay, I have been,
Trapped within the void unseen.
Light is distant in the cave,
Yet still it flickers, fierce and brave.

Let them in, these souls that care—
No kin, no blood, yet still they bear
The weight of woe, the burden grim,
To lift thee up when light grows dim.

A parchment white, a quill doth wait,
Send forth thy grief, unlock thy gate.
Or if thy lips dare speak, then say—
"988" shall light thy way.

For life, dear soul, is fragile, bright,
And darkness yields, if thou dost fight.

# 4

## WHISPERS TO THE MOON

### I. Patiently Waiting

Upon this hollow, waiting earth,
Where restless winds do wander wide,
I stand in silence—love's own birth,
A tide that swells, yet bides the tide.

No hurried hands, no pleading sigh,
For time, like death, must have its due.
The dawn shall break, the sun must rise,
Yet not before its hour is true.

O drink, my love, when thou dost crave,
This chalice full, this heart so deep.
No chains I forge, no fate I grave,
I wait—soft-shadowed, lost in sleep.

## II. My Amaterasu

From wretched gloom, from cavern deep,
Where specters whisper, shadows creep,
I roamed a ghost of ashen hue,
Till light, till thee—my sun broke through.

Thy gaze did strike like sacred fire,
A golden blade 'gainst fate's conspire.
And lo, I burned, yet not to die,
But rise, reborn, beneath thine eye.

Yet even stars do wane and fall,
Their fire fades, their embers small—
Tell me, sweet sun, dost thou still see
The flame thou once ignited in me?

## III. A Bee's Devotion

Do they whisper my name in the hush of the night?
Do they speak of my words in the glow of the light?
Do they jest at my longing, or question my ways—
How all that I do is a hymn to thy gaze?

Dost thou shun me for another's embrace?
Or is it mere shadows that darken my place?
No stage nor veil dost thou perform behind,
Yet still, I wonder—art thou truly mine?

Let us gather 'neath the moon's soft glow,
Share the flame where embers grow.
For I was lost in abyss untamed,
Till thy light through darkness came.

Once my heart sought beauty base,
Shallow pleasures, fleeting grace—
Yet thy smile, like dawn anew,
Turned my eyes from such a view.

A spell thou weavest, yet unaware,
A whisper soft, a tender snare.
If only thou couldst see thine worth,
Through mine eyes, thy heaven on earth.

I wait for thee, with patient grace,
Like a bee 'fore blossoms' embrace.
Savoring nectar, longing still,
Bound by love, by fate, by will.

### IV. The Confession

Do whispers of mine haunt thy breath?
Do echoes stir within thy chest?
Or have the tides that bound us tight
Withdrawn into the grasp of night?

Is it their tongues that weave thy mind?
Or dost thou flee to one unkind?
Thine absence lingers, keen and cold,
A tale of love left pale and old.

Once I gazed upon thy face,
And beauty's curse took hold my soul.
Lost within thy cruel embrace,
I drowned, I burned—I was made whole.

Thou lendest me a strength unearned,
A solace I had never known.
Yet still thy gaze from mine is turned,
And still I stand, a wretch alone.

Would that thou couldst wear mine eyes,
And see thee as the gods have willed.
For in thy form all heaven lies,
And in thy breath my wounds are stilled.

Thou speakest thus, thy heart undone,
Love's ruin sown in days now past.
Yet love, like ghosts, is never gone—
It lingers still, it holds thee fast.

And so I wait, through storm and tide,
A phantom locked in fate's cruel door.
No voice to beg, no will to chide,
But thine, and thine alone, once more.

Take thy time, love—fate may sever,
Yet here I stay—forever, ever.

# 5

## THE TYRANNY OF THY SMILE

No jewel nor gilded star above,
Could rival thee, my light, my love.
For in thy smile, a tempest sways,
A beacon lost in golden haze.

I wander lost, yet wish not flight,
A captive bound in soft delight.
The world recedes, fades into air,
When thou dost smile—a vision rare.

O cruel enchantress, dost thou see?
What power thy laughter holds o'er me?
A tyrant fair, yet sweetly wrought,
A peril, yet a cherished thought.

The savage tides within me quell,
A whisper soft, a broken spell.
And should thine eyes meet another's gaze,
My heart would burn in jealous blaze.

A narcotic deep, thy smile doth weave,
A dream from which I shan't retrieve.

# 6

# A HEART THAT WAITS

In silent hours, when moonlight wanes,
I whisper thoughts thou shalt not feign.
A specter soft, thy voice remains,
A balm to soothe my old refrains.

No tempest roars within my chest,
For thou hast bid the storm to rest.
With but a glance, my wrath is slain,
And in its stead, doth peace remain.

O radiant one, dost thou not see?
The world holds naught but dust to me.
Its hollow forms, its fleeting light—
They fade when thou art in my sight.

No golden crown, nor gem, nor throne,
Could match the love I long to own.
Not wealth, nor stars, nor kingdoms vast,
But thee, and thee alone, steadfast.

I know not well the art of speech,
Yet in thy presence, truths I reach.
For thou hast shaped the man I seek,
And taught my heart to feel and speak.

A love once foreign, now so near,
A bond untainted, pure, sincere.
To hold thee close, to guard thy grace,
To banish shadows from thy face.

Dost fear, my love, what fate may weave?
That time may take, that I may grieve?
Nay—let it twist, let moments turn,
Still here I stand, still here I yearn.

For patience deep, my soul hath learned,
A steadfast flame, unscorched, unburned.
The world may claim this heart of mine,
Yet loyalty remains but thine.

So when the hour calls thee true,
When doubts dissolve like morning dew,
Know this, my love, my solemn plea:
No chains bind thee—save love from me.

# 7

# A SMILE BEYOND THE VOID

In midnight musings, lost in thought,
A shadowed dream of thee is wrought.
O beauty fair, both dark and bright,
A beacon in the endless night.

Thy laughter lingers, soft yet bold,
A warmth that keeps the night from cold.
And in thy presence, doubts take flight,
Like phantoms banished by the light.

Yet in thy smile, so rare, so true,
I glimpse a world I never knew.
A place where wretches rise above,
Transformed by grace, consumed by love.

O how I tremble, weak, undone—
A weary soul, a wayward one.
For thou art fierce, a fire untamed,
And I, a man by sorrow maimed.

I laugh, I jest, I wear my guise,
Yet long to see through thy disguise.
For in thy depths, thy perfect scars,
Lies beauty greater than the stars.

But time is cruel, and fate unkind,
And fear doth plague my troubled mind.
For love once scorned leaves ruin deep,
A wound that wakes when others sleep.

And so, I watch, yet dare not speak,
A fleeting glance, a moment meek.
For thou, my heart, my phantom pain,
Art light that soothes—but brings me bane.

Yet still, if ever darkness calls,
And all the world around thee falls,
Know this, my love, my solemn vow:
I shall be near—I am thine now!

# PART II

## THE SHADOW

### LETTERS I NEVER MEANT TO WRITE (BUT ALWAYS FELT)

**8**

---

# YOU SAY YOU LOVE ME, BUT...

You say you love me—
but only when the ache of distance wraps
its hands around your throat,
when silence feels like abandonment,
and loneliness turns my absence into a wound.

But what if I told you—
these connections you clutch so tightly,
the ones you weave into meaning,
mean nothing to me?

Because guess what...
You weren't there when I needed you.
So I cried to someone else—twice.

Once for the pain I carried alone,
twice for the weight of knowing
you were the one meant to hold me up.

I've learned your stories,
memorized the way you play the victim,
but I could never shake the hatred
for the way you make me the villain.

You say it hurts that I "feel like" I have to talk to others—
but that's like throwing up without tasting the bitterness.

Would we even be here
if you had just done your job?

I'm tired—
tired of questioning if I'm the bad one,
tired of making space for excuses
that shrink me into someone unrecognizable.

Yeah, I've made mistakes too,
but here's the difference between me and you:
I would never set out to hurt you.
I would never make you feel small.

But you did.
And when the dust settled,
you buried me in lies,
watered my name with whispers
to those too blind to question you.

And somehow—somehow,
I still grew.

## 9

# THE FLOWER AND THE BEE

Flowers—silent, radiant, strong—
standing tall with roots deep and sure,
they bloom in the right embrace,
in soil that knows how to love them.

And oh, if only we could be like the bees,
drawn not to waste but to sweetness,
never needing to explain why honey
is richer than rot.

I would never ask a bee to settle
for a tree or a bush—
it knows where the nectar flows best.

And we, without knowing,
sip their golden labor,
finding something oddly satisfying
in what was once their toil.

But this poem isn't just about bees,
or flowers,
or the foundations we build—
it's about a single bloom
that never left my mind.

You may not call it the fairest,
but the Tiger Lily has always been mine,
the only flower worthy
of holding the beauty
I remember from all those years ago.

Flowers have many purposes—
to bloom, to wither, to be reborn.

And if beauty is in the eye of the beholder,
then let my eyes
and my mind be yours to hold.

# 10

## AN OBJECT OF MY FEELINGS

I think my issue is—I crave connection,
a kind of tether beyond words,
where I get lost in your eyes,
biting my lip at the way you move,
at the way you simply exist.

I want to be free in my admiration,
to trace the elegance of your beauty
without fear of being called needy or too much.

I don't want to ration my love—
I want to pour it over you like sunlight,
knowing you'll soak it in,
knowing it's enough.

I want to tell you how I feel
and hear your words wrap around me,
convincing me I'm safe,
that I'm not alone in this.

I want to make you cry—
but only in the best ways,
only when my love
fills your eyes like morning dew,
only when the weight of my affection
presses against your heart so sweetly
that it overflows.

I want to hold you,
long enough to get dizzy
from how amazing you smell,
long enough to forget
where your heartbeat ends and mine begins.

I want to give you everything—
without demand, without obligation.

Love that is love, not transaction.

I'm tired of feeling like I love too much,
like my heart is a flood
no one can swim in.

I want to drown in you—
in warmth, in laughter,
in the way your cuddles
outmatch the cold side of my pillow.

And if my touch is too much,
if my hands speak louder than my words,

*Letters I Never Meant to Write (But Always Felt)*

know that I would never make you an object—
unless we agree that you are
an object of my feelings,
a vessel for the love
I've been afraid to give.

So let's take this dive,
headfirst into the oven of love,
and hope we drown—
only in each other.

## 11

## A GIFT FROM MORPHEUS

Lord Morpheus, Dream King,
must have a fondness for me—

for when I closed my eyes last night,
he placed in my hands
the sweetest gift a mortal could receive.

I dreamed of you. And it felt so real, so sweet,
so agonizingly intimate—
because I knew, eventually, I would wake.

Wake to a world
where your perfume doesn't stir butterflies in my chest,
where your twinkling eyes are just a memory,
where we do not lie in the grass,
wrapped in each other,
whispering wishes to the stars.

A world where I do not gaze at them at all—
because how could I care for distant lights

when your smile shines brighter,
when I hold my breath between blinks,
too afraid to miss even a second
of your beauty?

If I were a fish,
I'd wish you to be my gills—
then maybe I'd have an answer to Jordin Sparks' question:
*How am I supposed to breathe with no air?*

Because that's how I feel when you're not here.

I would not call you a drug—
addiction is too real—
but if there's a high in this world that doesn't need chasing,
it must be you.

Yet as I wake,
I wonder if Morpheus laughs, knowing my fate—
that no dream, no fantasy,
could ever compare to the agony
of loving you from afar.

# A LOVE MISPLACED

I accidentally fell for you yesterday—
yes, indeed, it's true.
I swore I'd rather be alone at night,
but now my days are filled with you.

Daydreams spill like waves on shore,
laughs and walks replay in loops,
a wonderland delight where we are lost together—
just us two.

Who knew a feeling could be this deep,
as boundless as the ocean's blue?
Yet in my fairytale of love,
the only creatures here are thoughts of you.

At first, you lingered in the corner,
barely more than passing light—
until the day I saw it clear,
that I had fallen, lost in flight.

And when I learned I couldn't have you,
the world could burn for all I cared—
my heart ripped out, yet you weren't to blame,
for I had left it unprepared.

So now it's back to square one,
where silence builds a quiet wall.
Marcus Houston sings me through it,
but his words can't break my fall.

I hold on tight to angles sharp,
refusing circles, endless, cruel—
for if you are not within my orbit,
then what's the point of spinning through?

# 13

## THE POETRY OF LOVE

In English, we say *I love you*—
but in poetry, we confess:
My heart feels deprived of you,
skipping a beat
each time my eyes meet yours.

Once, I lived without knowing you.
Now, the thought of losing you
brings tears I cannot hide.

Your time, your attention, your presence—
they are not just gifts,
but blessings I dare not take for granted.

I would give the food from my mouth
just to see you eat,
for I know my love alone
may never be enough.

To truly desire someone—
to feel their absence like a missing piece—
is the greatest, most terrifying truth.

You once asked my favorite pastime
before we were bound as one.
It used to be reading, writing,
simply existing in my world.

But now?
Now, my greatest joy is consuming your time—
and praying that you, in turn,
consume mine.

## 14

# LOVESTRUCK IN THE SARANGETTI

Through thick and thin, I'll always stay—
love you, I do, come what may.
Despite what whispers the world might share,
my heart is yours, laid fully bare.

Like rivers through the Serengeti's bones,
where all seems dry, where silence moans—
until the animals stir, revived by grace—
that's my love, flowing through empty space.

Or like a catfish deep in mud,
waiting patiently for the rain's soft thud,
I lie in stillness, heart unshown,
yet holding breath, not quite alone.

I'd trade places with gators in the heat,
traveling hellfire just for a single meet—
risking being cooked in the cruel sun's flame,
if it meant whispering once more your name.

The metaphor may wobble, the logic stray,
but the feeling? It's real, in every way.
So like the desert waits for rain's return,
and flowers bloom where fire once burned—
I'll wait for you, through storm or shine,
to bring new life to this lovestruck mind.

# 1 FISH, 2 FISH, LOVE LIKE THIS

1 fish, 2 fish, red fish, blue—
but none could match the depths of you.

My love's a buffet, full and grand,
1 dish, 2 dish, made by hand.
Red dish of passion, blue dish of peace,
each bite of us a sweet release.

I want our love to move like sound—
a Ne-Yo song, slow and profound.
The kind that lingers, clings to skin,
like perfume worn from deep within.

A scent that sings of where you've been,
etched in my breath again and again.
You light my pheromones on fire,
a spark that climbs and won't retire.

I could find you in an endless tide,
by scent alone, I'd stand with pride.

I'll do anything—anything true—
to not become Vic Fuentes too.

My love, once bulletproof and bright,
but pierced by you in silent night.
Still, I'd wear the wound if it meant
I'd once been wrapped in your sweet scent.

So 1 love, 2 love, deep as the sea—
just say the word, and come to me.

# 16

## SHAKESPEARE WITHOUT THE TRAGEDY

I want a love that's Shakespearean—
just without the tragic end.
A tale not written in sorrow,
but in joy that never bends.

A love so strong it quiets storms,
a peace born deep in passion's forms.

And should the world collapse,
unravel at the seams,
I vow to guard the truth of us,
to cherish all your dreams.

My love is pure, my love is true—
and even if we part,
my love stays with you.

You make me sing at the top of my lungs,
like One Direction taught me when I was young:
*"If only you saw what I can see,"*
then you'd know why you mean the world to me.

You don't know you're beautiful—and that's the thing—
it's in your smile, your laugh, the joy you bring.

And that hair? That perfect, messy bun—
it hits my chest like a rising sun.
Like Harry said, *"the way you flip your hair"*—
I swear, it takes away my air.

Every song I write, each lyric true,
it starts with me just thinking of you.

If we were music, we'd share one sound,
same frequency, same wave,
the same heart-pounding ground.

### *Letters I Never Meant to Write (But Always Felt)*

Tunnel vision takes over when you're near,
the world falls silent—only you I hear.

I don't know if this is what soulmates do—
but I know I've never felt this way before you.

You filled a space I never knew was hollow,
a wholeness I'm still learning to follow.

Like gravity through the fabric of space,
you pull me in with timeless grace.

When we dance, when we touch,
when we walk hand in hand,
I swear I feel the universe finally understand.

Yes, it's true—I have feelings for you,
so let this flame of emotion burn honest and new.

For in this life or the next, I will always choose
to be the light that never lets the fire lose.

My one true love, my reason, my rhyme—
the soul I searched for across all time.

# 17

## HIGHLIGHT ME IN YOUR STORY

I have a favorite everything when it comes to you—
a favorite laugh, a favorite look, a favorite "what you do."

Even your quirks, your awkward moments,
your silent stares and loud components—
they all made their way into my list.
Even your cringe has a spot I wouldn't dare resist.

Because I like you for you—even the things you hide
or try to brush off when you get tongue-tied.

That's the magic of real connection.
It's not perfection—it's reflection.
The little details that make you whole,
the scattered pieces that complete your soul.

I remember fearing I'd never find someone quite like you.
And then it hit me—
I won't.
And that's okay too.

You see, life is made of chapters and turns,
of bridges crossed and lessons learned.
Not everyone makes it to the final page,
but their presence still echoes across the stage.

Even if we drift and part before the end,
I'll cherish every moment we didn't have to pretend.

So if this was our last chapter and we never knew,
just do me one favor, simple and true—
highlight your favorite paragraphs of me.
The ones where you smiled, the ones you felt free.

And I'll take my pen and with steady hand,
write you a story of how a toe-touch from heaven
fell into my land.

A tale of you—
the perfect blessing the gods chose to send,
even if you weren't meant to stay 'til the end.

## 18

## RECESSIVE RADIANCE

You see, I've never been drawn to redheads—
until you.

Something about you makes me lose my mind,
like gravity shifted and your presence redefined
what beauty means in my eyes.

They say red hair is a recessive trait,
but I say it's a miracle of fate.
A rare bloom in a field of sameness,
proof that something unexpected can still be ageless.

Those freckles? Tiny constellations on your skin.
Your hair? Already the masterpiece others dye to begin.

Your eyes? Lit like autumn skies right before dusk,
that hue that dances between fire and trust.

You call it recessive—
I call it divine.

A rare spark in the bloodline
that somehow made its way to you
to show the world something beautifully true.

You remind me of the seasons shifting,
pumpkin spice and leaves drifting.
You search for dying colors with eager eyes,
because you know even endings can wear a beautiful disguise.

That's why I say you're "stuffy on the eyes"—
because you take my breath,
like watching the sunset and knowing
it's the day's gentle death.

But beauty still clings to its final light.
Even in darkness, it learns how to fight.

So when you're feeling dim,
like you're hidden within—
think of Amaterasu, the sun goddess in lore,
who hid herself when chaos shook her core.

The world turned black in her silent stay,
until laughter and dancing called her back to day.

So if ever you forget how to shine,
dance. Laugh. Even if you're alone with the divine.
Because even the gods needed a reason to rise—
and yours?
It's written in your freckles,
your fire-touched hair,
and the way you teach the world how to care.

# PART III

## THE SILENCE

ECHOES OF PRINCIPLE: A RECKONING
WITH THE PAST

## 19

# A PHILOSOPHER'S FIRST LAMENT: LOVE AND LOSS

It was meant to be you—
or so the heart once whispered in its longing.
Yet the fates, indifferent weavers,
never spun such a thread for us.

I have unlearned you time and time again,
each lesson carved in sorrow,
each farewell a fire that scorched my soul.
Hell itself would marvel at such torment.

And when you returned, so, too, did an old companion—
not joy, not peace, but the knowing.

The knowing that love would rise anew
only to be left to die in your absence.

What name does this sorrow bear?
It clings to me,
as if woven into my very skin,
stitched with threads of foolish hope.

I have barred the door to your return,
locked it not for your sake,
but for my own—
for I grew weary of wielding the knife
that tore my own heart asunder.

And now, I watch from a distance,
as you bind your life to the one you once scorned,
dreaming of children in the arms
that you swore were not enough.

Yet here I sit,
accepting the love I believe I deserve—
or so the saying goes.

You were the first to show me
that my heart is vast enough for the world,
but my loyalty was always meant for one.

And yet—
you were never the one to whom I spoke those words.

Still, I thank you.
For you have gifted me the cruelest wisdom,
one that life so often bestows
on those who love too deeply—
a lesson wrapped in loss,
a truth carried in silence.

# 20

# A PHILOSOPHER'S MEDITATION ON DUTY AND DESIRE

I never sought for things to unravel so.
My desire was simple—change,
heed, align.

Yet perhaps therein lies my flaw,
for in my eyes, I held mere expectations,
and in the world's eyes,
I was a force too rigid, too demanding.

Why, then, do so many falter beneath these expectations?
Why does disappointment tread so often in my wake?

Is it I who errs, or they who lack resolve?
Tell me—
am I the tyrant of my own design,
a storm that commands yet never yields?

If so, then let it be known—
I have never asked for worship,
only the dignity of respect.

A man of principle—
should he not be bound to honor?
Or is it principle itself that binds
and drags one into the depths of consequence?

For me, principle is no shackle,
but a flame-retardant against folly,
a shield against deception's reach.

Yet so often, I find myself in battle—
not against falsehood,
but against those who wield their emotions
as if they were the law itself.

They speak as if feeling should undo my reason,
as if sentiment alone should fracture truth.

And yet, their arrogance does not bend me—
it steels me,
driving me deeper into the sanctuary of logic,
into the unyielding arms of principle.

Let them call it harshness.
Let them call it cold.
But let them never say that I swayed without cause.

## 21

---

# A PHILOSOPHER'S RECKONING WITH BETRAYAL

I will not mask my words, nor dress them in pleasantries.
For what use is civility when truth itself stands defiled?

You—
a cunning, selfish specter of deceit,
woven from threads of disrespect and disregard.

It is not mere anger that binds me to this resentment,
but the principle,
unyielding as stone,
a truth I cannot unsee,
nor forgive.

But perhaps, in these words, there lies a small mercy—
a space where I may speak without the weight of finance,
without the chain of judgment,

without the expectation
that every thought must end in battle.

And yet, tell me—
who are you to dictate
the boundaries of my feelings?
To twist inquiry into accusation?
To cry of wounds,
while wielding the blade yourself?

I am no sage,
but even a fool knows
when the world stinks of falsehood.

Your hypocrisy drips from your words,
your contradictions scatter like broken glass.

Lacking in empathy, void of compassion,
you cast judgment upon me
even as you drown in your own reflection.

And for what?
To shield yourself from the weight of your own failings?
To twist my longing into betrayal,
accusing me of sins you scarcely understand?

I could list your transgressions,
count them like coins,
build a fortune from the wreckage of our past.

But wealth holds no candle
to the shame I hope festers within you—

the simple truth that all you ever needed
was a fraction of maturity,
a whisper of accountability.

Yet here I stand, watching the ruins,
knowing that for every wrong you inflicted,
it was I who was left to mend,
to clean,
to follow in the wake
of your careless destruction.

I do not deny my flaws.
But if you cast me as the villain,
then so be it.

I will wear the role you have written for me,
for at least in this story—
I stand in truth.

**22**

---

# A PHILOSOPHER'S FAREWELL
# TO LOVE

It was meant to be you—
or so the heart once whispered in its longing.
Yet the fates, indifferent weavers,
never spun such a thread for us.

I have unlearned you time and time again,
each lesson carved in sorrow,
each farewell a fire that scorched my soul.
Hell itself would marvel at such torment.

And when you returned, so, too, did an old companion—
not joy, not peace, but the knowing.

The knowing that love would rise anew
only to be left to die in your absence.

What name does this sorrow bear?
It clings to me,
as if woven into my very skin,
stitched with threads of foolish hope.

I have barred the door to your return,
locked it not for your sake,
but for my own—
for I grew weary of wielding the knife
that tore my own heart asunder.

And now, I watch from a distance,
as you bind your life to the one you once scorned,
dreaming of children in the arms
that you swore were not enough.

Yet here I sit,
accepting the love I believe I deserve—
or so the saying goes.

You were the first to show me
that my heart is vast enough for the world,
but my loyalty was always meant for one.

And yet—
you were never the one to whom I spoke those words.

Still, I thank you.
For you have gifted me the cruelest wisdom,
one that life so often bestows
on those who love too deeply—
a lesson wrapped in loss,
a truth carried in silence.

# 23

## A PHILOSOPHER'S RECKONING WITH MORAL DEBT

I never sought for things to unravel so.
My desire was simple—change,
heed, align.

Yet perhaps therein lies my flaw,
for in my eyes, I held mere expectations,
and in the world's eyes,
I was a force too rigid, too demanding.

Why, then, do so many falter beneath these expectations?
Why does disappointment tread so often in my wake?

Is it I who errs, or they who lack resolve?
Tell me—
am I the tyrant of my own design,
a storm that commands yet never yields?

If so, then let it be known—
I have never asked for worship,
only the dignity of respect.

A man of principle—
should he not be bound to honor?
Or is it principle itself that binds
and drags one into the depths of consequence?

For me, principle is no shackle,
but a flame-retardant against folly,
a shield against deception's reach.

Yet so often, I find myself in battle—
not against falsehood,
but against those who wield their emotions
as if they were the law itself.

They speak as if feeling should undo my reason,
as if sentiment alone should fracture truth.

And yet, their arrogance does not bend me—
it steels me,
driving me deeper into the sanctuary of logic,
into the unyielding arms of principle.

Let them call it harshness.
Let them call it cold.
But let them never say that I swayed without cause.

## 24

---

# A PHILOSOPHER'S LETTER TO THE BETRAYER

I will not mask my words, nor dress them in pleasantries.
For what use is civility when truth itself stands defiled?

You—
a cunning, selfish specter of deceit,
woven from threads of disrespect and disregard.

It is not mere anger that binds me to this resentment,
but the principle, unyielding as stone,
a truth I cannot unsee,
nor forgive.

But perhaps, in these words,
there lies a small mercy—
a space where I may speak
without the weight of finance,
without the chain of judgment,
without the expectation
that every thought must end in battle.

And yet, tell me—
who are you to dictate
the boundaries of my feelings?
To twist inquiry into accusation?
To cry of wounds,
while wielding the blade yourself?

I am no sage,
but even a fool knows
when the world stinks of falsehood.

Your hypocrisy drips from your words,
your contradictions scatter like broken glass.

Lacking in empathy,
void of compassion,
you cast judgment upon me
even as you drown in your own reflection.

And for what?
To shield yourself from the weight of your own failings?
To twist my longing into betrayal,
accusing me of sins you scarcely understand?

I could list your transgressions,
count them like coins,
build a fortune from the wreckage of our past.

But wealth holds no candle
to the shame I hope festers within you—

*Echoes of Principle: A Reckoning with the Past*

the simple truth that all you ever needed
was a fraction of maturity,
a whisper of accountability.

Yet here I stand, watching the ruins,
knowing that for every wrong you inflicted,
it was I who was left to mend,
to clean,
to follow in the wake
of your careless destruction.

I do not deny my flaws.
But if you cast me as the villain, then so be it.

I will wear the role you have written for me—
for at least in this story,
I stand in truth.

# 25

# A PHILOSOPHER'S SOLILOQUY ON ILLUSIONS AND CLOSURE

Though these words may never reach you,
and if they do,
they will not stir you without another's whispers in your ear,
still, I write them.

Not as an attack,
not as a revelation—
for you have long since unveiled the truth yourself.

The tragedy is not in your deception,
but in my blindness—
in my refusal to see the colors you bled so freely before me.

So many dreams left unpursued,
so many paths abandoned,
all in the name of sacrifice,
all in the hope that my devotion might sculpt your happiness.

And yet, what remains?

Disappointment and heartache, carved into my bones,
while you tell me it was never enough,
while you place the weight of failure upon my shoulders.

What wounds me more?
The years squandered on a dream,
a fragile illusion of us,
or the bitter thought that your love may have been
nothing more than a well-rehearsed performance?

I gather the fragments you left behind,
a puzzle shattered before the box was even opened,
a game rigged before the first move was made.

You were always three steps ahead,
hidden in your secrecy,
leaving me grasping at shadows.

But now, I have a plan of my own.
And when it unfolds, smooth as a napkin in an idle hand,
you will stand in silence,
bewildered,
while I—
perhaps for the first time—
will breathe in the still air of peace.

Call it petty, if you must.
I am no stranger to rising above.
But even the most disciplined hand
can slip in the dance of retribution.

# 26

# A PHILOSOPHER'S QUIET WAR: ON CONFLICT AND PEACE

I do not revel in ultimatums,
yet they seem the only keys
to unlocking your will
from the prison of self-interest.

Still, I am cast as the aggressor,
though force is the only tongue
that seems to move you toward fairness.

Yes—
I know my faults,
as you know yours,
yet we have both chosen comfort over confrontation,
sweeping grievances under the rug
until we trip over the pile.

And so I wonder, as I always do,
if all of this could have been spared
had I simply been cruel
instead of patient.

Respect was all I asked.
Love was all you required.
Yet we rationed them, holding out like misers—
each withholding
for lack of receiving.

Still, I search for the moment
when our mutual respect vanished,
slipping away like wind-carried ash,
leaving only the scent of what once was.

But in writing, I find release.
I cast the hate from my heart,
letting it spill from my veins
so it may no longer poison me.

I regret nothing,
save for the order of my choices.
I took the risks you feared,
and in the end,
they did not break me—
only stained me,
like ink spilled from a dying squid,
a darkness that lingers,
waiting only for the right light
to wash it away.

Perhaps my failing
was in forgetting the balance—

between now and the future,
between ambition and presence.

And for that, I have faltered.
For that, I will bear the weight.
But never will I regret
the act of reaching beyond fear.

# 27

## A PHILOSOPHER'S LAMENT ON CYCLES AND UNCERTAINTY

I have learned to loathe our conversations,
for each word from your lips
pulls me back into the same familiar abyss—
a high school heart,
naïve and hopeful,
only to be abandoned once more,
a ghost left in your wake.

And so I wonder—
do you take pleasure in this torment?
Do you see the pattern,
or am I alone in my suffering?

I tire of these partings,
these illusions of finality.
Each farewell feels like the last,
until you return,
like an echo in an empty hall,
like an affliction I cannot shake.

If hatred fuels your return,
or if you still feel as I do,
I may never know.

But you always come back,
lingering like an itch,
a presence I wish to erase.

Perhaps these words will find you one day,
and you will remember—
the pink hoodie I gifted you,
the moments that once felt infinite.

Perhaps we were never meant to be.
Perhaps I was simply never meant for you.

But the answer will remain a whisper,
a question lost to time,
forever unresolved.

**28**

# A PHILOSOPHER'S REFLECTION ON JUSTICE AND CLOSURE

What troubles me about double standards and the nature of self-
importance
is how they seem to shift only when wielded against men.

We walk within a world where goodness is not enough,
where virtue is weighed and twisted,
where truth is not a shield
but a weapon repurposed against its bearer.

And for that, I pity you—
for the mirror you refuse to face,
for the blindness of ego
that shields you from your own reflection.

Time, ever patient,
will unveil your true colors.
And though I should be above it,
I find solace in knowing
that the life you have crafted
will one day answer for itself.

Yet only those who see themselves in these words
will take offense.
Only those who fit the shape
will bristle at its outline.

But anger no longer burdens me.
This is not an invitation.
This is not a door left ajar.
You have shown me all that I needed to see—
more than I ever wished to know.

And so I leave you with this:
As Kevin Hart once said,
"Everything I could do, I did.
Everything I couldn't do, I tried."

May life grant you exactly what you deserve.